B. Tiepolo.

D.D Velasquez.

Guercamp M.

H. Rousseau

P Gauguin

Fran.co Dezurbaran 1639

C. Pissarro 1872

Paolo Veronese

John Constable

ant. Watteau.

M. Robbema 1662

This book is designed for use both in the National Gallery and at home.

There are some pages of questions which you will find much easier to answer if you are standing (or sitting) in front of the actual paintings.

Room numbers have not been mentioned because the pictures are sometimes moved. If you have any difficulty in finding a particular painting, ask one of the attendants.

If your visit to the Gallery can only be a short one, don't worry. There is plenty in this book for you to do at home. This homing pigeon will show you which pages are easiest to do at home.

Please remember never to get too close to a painting and never to touch one.

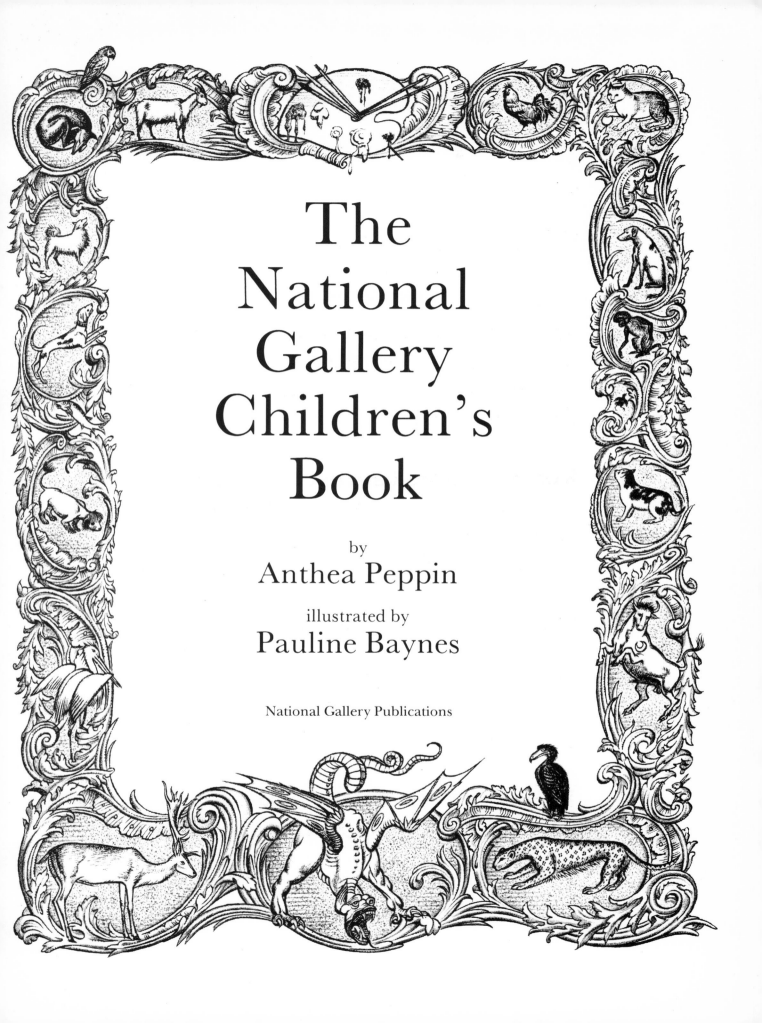

The National Gallery Children's Book

by
Anthea Peppin

illustrated by
Pauline Baynes

National Gallery Publications

First Published 1983. Reprinted 1985, 1989, 1990, 1992, 1993

NGPL Stock Number 525044

ISBN 0 901791 90 3

Edited and designed by Faith Brabenec Hart

Calligraphy and picture research by Sarah Brown
Tiger cut-out by Brigid Curtis

PHOTOGRAPHIC ACKNOWLEDGEMENTS

Tulip vase reproduced by gracious permission of Her Majesty the Queen

Full-size sketch for *The Hay Wain*, *Study of Clouds* and *Study of Cirrus Clouds* by John Constable reproduced by courtesy of the Victoria and Albert Museum (Crown Copyright)

Wilton House courtesy of the British Tourist Authority

Laocoön courtesy of the Mansell Collection

Cartoon No. 1, *Punch*, 1843

Photograph of Willy Lott's Cottage by Eileen Graham

Printed by Grosvenor Press (Portsmouth) Ltd.

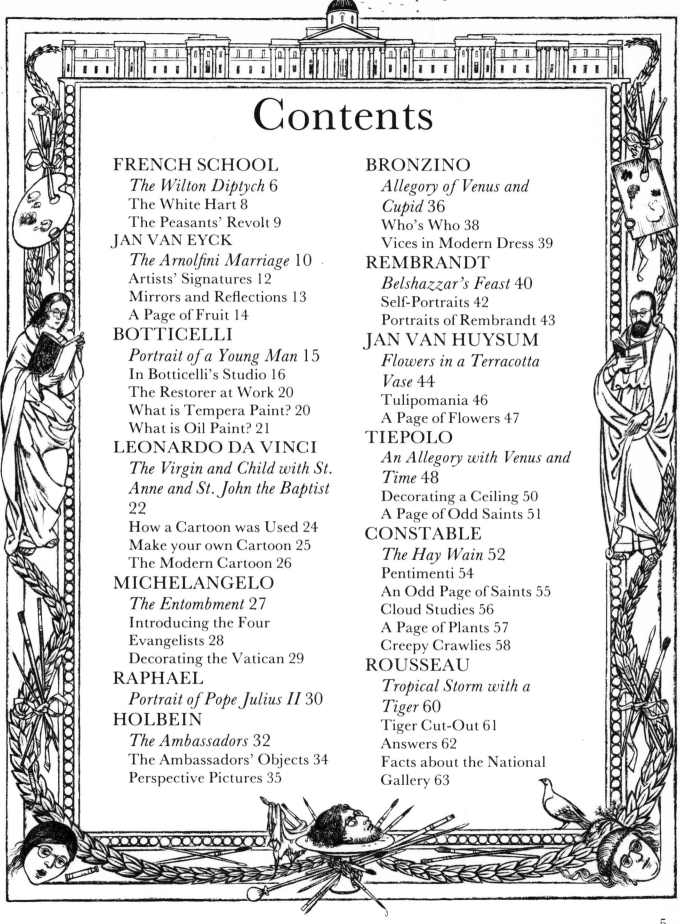

Contents

FRENCH SCHOOL

This is King Richard II of England.

He reigned from the year 1377 until 1399 when he was forced to abdicate. He died in 1400 at the age of 33.

How old was he when he became King? _____ (Do a sum and work it out.)

The three men standing behind the King are his patron saints. They are presenting him to the Virgin and Child on the other half of the painting.

Look carefully at Richard's necklace – it is made of pods of a plant called BROOM (rather like pea pods). Broom was one of Richard's family emblems – you can see it in the pattern on his robes too.

Where else in the picture can you see Broom Pods?

_____

6

(If you are in the Gallery, don't forget to look at the back of the painting.)

The Wilton Diptych

The sky is real gold – beaten very thin and stuck on. The blue is made from a semi-precious stone (called LAPIS LAZULI) which was ground to powder and used as paint. Lapis lazuli was even more expensive than gold when this picture was painted – so the cost must have been enormous.

The picture is called the *Wilton Diptych*, because it used to be at Wilton House in Wiltshire. The artist is not known, but he was probably French.

Wilton House

The white hart (a male deer which has grown its antlers) was the emblem of King Richard himself. How many badges like this one are there? _____

Richard's family name was PLANTAGENET. *Genet* is French for Broom. *Planta* means plant. So he was really Richard Broomplant!

Look at the baby's halo. How is the gold decorated?

with rose buds? _____
with rays of light? _____
with prickly thorns? _____

7

The White Hart

Here is King Richard II's White Hart.
Trace it. Then draw a garden or forest around it.

The Peasants' Revolt

(Here is a true story about Richard II for you to colour.)

In the year 1381 large numbers of poor peasants marched from Kent to London to protest against a new tax they had to pay. Their leader was Wat Tyler.

They stormed into the city and burnt all the records they could find. The King, Richard II, was only 14 at the time. He agreed to meet the rebels at Mile End.

While some rebels met the King, others broke into the Tower of London, where they killed the archbishop and the treasurer, whom they blamed for the tax.

On the next day Richard II rode out to meet the rebels at Smithfield. This time Wat Tyler was so rude that the King's followers killed him.

Bravely the king rode up to the rebels and persuaded them to follow him. He led them away from London and sent them home with free pardons.

But later the young King's advisors persuaded him to change his mind, and the remaining leaders of the revolt were tried and executed.

JAN VAN EYCK

Jan Van Eyck worked in the town of Bruges in Flanders (now part of Belgium).
Find it on the map below.

We do not know the year of his birth, but he was active as a painter by 1422 and he died in 1441.

He was employed by the Duke of Burgundy, who sent him on secret missions to Spain and Portugal.

Until this time, most paintings were of religious subjects. However, in the fifteenth century portraits became fashionable.

Van Eyck was one of the first artists to use oil paints. (Before that they usually used tempera – see page 20.) These oil paints enabled him to get much richer effects of colour and light and shade. It was also a technique that helped the artist to put in very tiny details. Look carefully at this painting and answer the questions on the opposite page.

(In the Gallery REMEMBER . . . DON'T GET TOO CLOSE . . . DON'T POINT . . . AND NEVER, NEVER TOUCH A PAINTING.)

10

The Arnolfini Marriage

The couple in this picture are being married. (People got married at home quite often in those days.)

Do you think they are wearing their best clothes? _____

Do you think Van Eyck has tried to flatter these two people by making them extra beautiful? _____

Do they look:
pleased? _____
excited? _____
surprised? _____
hungry? _____
happy? _____
sleepy? _____
bored? _____
in love? _____
grumpy? _____
worried? _____
angry? _____
or what? _____

Where has the artist written his name on the painting? _____

Look at the circular convex mirror on the back wall. (Convex means that it curves outwards. The opposite of convex is concave.) The mirror shows a distorted view of the room.

How many people can you see reflected in it? _____

What do you think the mirror frame is made of? _____

The little scenes in the frame show the events of the last days of Christ's life on earth – the story of the Passion.

How many scenes are there? _____

Why do you think there is only one candle?
1. It is a candle clock? _____
2. It represents divine light because the ceremony is a holy one? _____
3. Or do you think it is impossible to say? _____

Is the candle alight? _____

Tick which of the following you can see (try to find 10):
nails in floorboards _____
lighted candle _____
prayer beads _____
brush _____
carpet _____
oranges _____
fruit bowl _____
window _____
dog's whiskers _____
clock _____
bed _____
tree _____

What sort of room is this?
chapel? _____
kitchen? _____
sitting room? _____
bedroom? _____
or what? _____

11

Artists' Signatures

Here is Jan Van Eyck's signature enlarged.
Try to trace it as carefully as you can.

It says: Johannes de eyck fuit hic
1434

It means: Jan Van Eyck was here
1434

Here is another grand signature by another artist
– Jan Van Huysum. Trace this one too.

(You can find out more about this artist later in this book.)

Now invent a really grand signature for yourself.
Make sure you practise it so that it always looks the same.

Mirrors and Reflections

Here is a mirror frame like the one in *The Arnolfini Marriage*.
Show a room from your home reflected in it.
Then add suitable decorations round the frame.
Put in lots of tiny details as Jan Van Eyck would have done.

A Page of Fruit

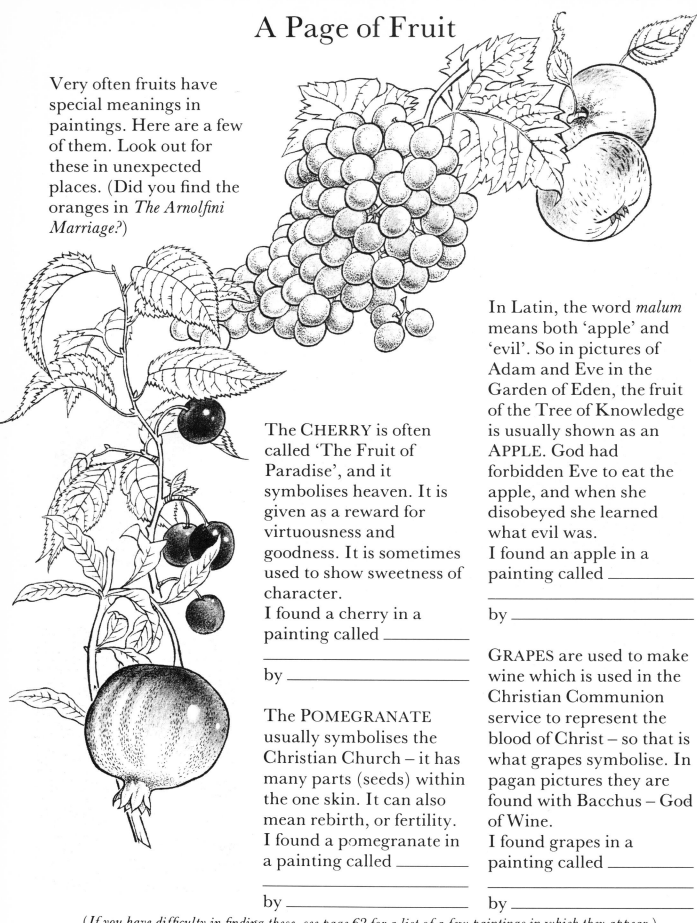

Very often fruits have special meanings in paintings. Here are a few of them. Look out for these in unexpected places. (Did you find the oranges in *The Arnolfini Marriage?*)

The CHERRY is often called 'The Fruit of Paradise', and it symbolises heaven. It is given as a reward for virtuousness and goodness. It is sometimes used to show sweetness of character.
I found a cherry in a painting called ＿＿＿＿＿

＿＿＿＿＿＿＿＿＿＿＿

by ＿＿＿＿＿＿＿＿＿

The POMEGRANATE usually symbolises the Christian Church – it has many parts (seeds) within the one skin. It can also mean rebirth, or fertility.
I found a pomegranate in a painting called ＿＿＿＿

＿＿＿＿＿＿＿＿＿＿＿

by ＿＿＿＿＿＿＿＿＿

In Latin, the word *malum* means both 'apple' and 'evil'. So in pictures of Adam and Eve in the Garden of Eden, the fruit of the Tree of Knowledge is usually shown as an APPLE. God had forbidden Eve to eat the apple, and when she disobeyed she learned what evil was.
I found an apple in a painting called ＿＿＿＿

＿＿＿＿＿＿＿＿＿＿＿

by ＿＿＿＿＿＿＿＿＿

GRAPES are used to make wine which is used in the Christian Communion service to represent the blood of Christ – so that is what grapes symbolise. In pagan pictures they are found with Bacchus – God of Wine.
I found grapes in a painting called ＿＿＿＿

＿＿＿＿＿＿＿＿＿＿＿

by ＿＿＿＿＿＿＿＿＿

(If you have difficulty in finding these, see page 62 for a list of a few paintings in which they appear.)

BOTTICELLI
Portrait of a Young Man

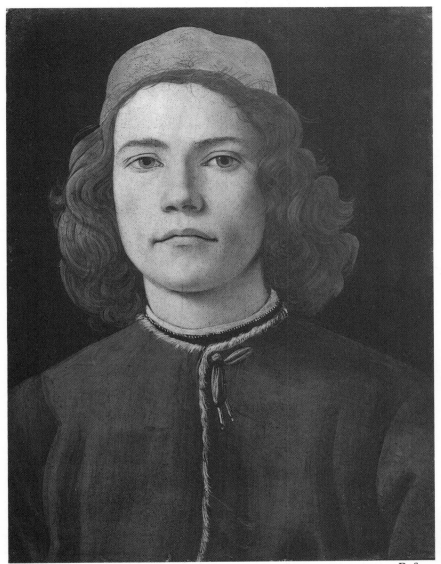

Before

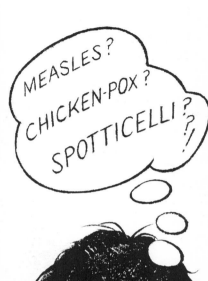

DID THIS YOUNG MAN REALLY HAVE MEASLES?

This photograph was taken before this painting was cleaned in 1968. It shows small black spots all over the young man's face.

Find the painting in the National Gallery and compare it with the old photograph.

Can you see any spots on the painting today? _____

After

15

IN BOTTICELLI'S STUDIO . . .

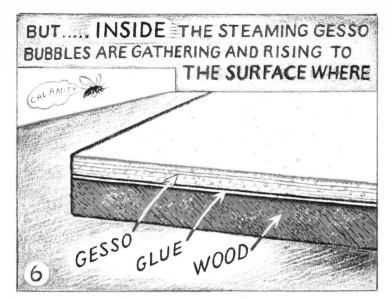

BUT..... **INSIDE** THE STEAMING GESSO BUBBLES ARE GATHERING AND RISING TO **THE SURFACE WHERE**

CALAMITY

GESSO GLUE WOOD

6

THEY **BURST**

POP POP POP POP POP

7 LEAVING TINY HOLES...

GLUE AND GESSO APPLIED AND DRIED.....

THE PANEL IS READY TO BE PAINTED

where's that dratted hen?

POP

8

WHY IS BOTTICELLI'S ASSISTANT OFF TO FIND THE HEN ? SEE PAGE 20 FOR EGGSPLANATION

FORTUNATELY

PHEW thank goodness the sizzling doesn't show when the paint is on

9

BUT LITTLE DID HE GUESS THAT IN A FEW HUNDRED YEARS DIRT WOULD COLLECT IN THOSE HOLES

10 EEEK ALL IS REVEALED

...AND BOTTICELLI'S PAINTING DEVELOPED SPOTS

The Restorer at Work

How and Why a Painting is Cleaned

Over the years, paintings become dark and discoloured by layers of dirt, and old varnish which has gradually turned brown.

Skilled restorers use tiny pieces of cotton wool dipped in solvents (for example, types of alcohol). These are gently rubbed on the picture surface. The old varnish dissolves and is mopped up by the cotton wool. The work must be done very slowly and carefully – inch by inch.

The restorer will also remove any later paint which does not belong to the original picture. (See page 37 for an example of this kind of OVERPAINTING.) In Botticelli's *Portrait of a Young Man* the restorer had to pick the dirt out of each small hole with a dentist's probe! It took a very long time.

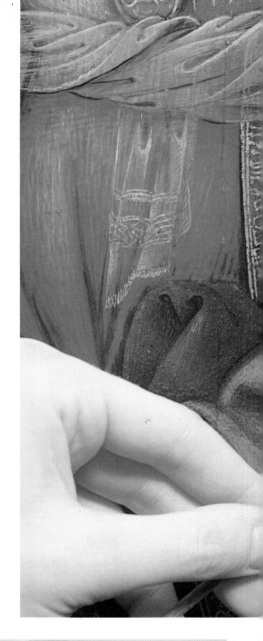

(*right*) The restorer uses a solvent on cotton wool to dissolve and remove old discoloured varnish.

(*below centre*) Often before a painting can be relined with new canvas, a previous relining has to be removed. This restorer is scraping off the old canvas relining and the glue that held it to the painting.

(*below far right*) The electrically heated hot table is being used to join a new canvas lining to the back of this old painting.

(*below*) The STEREO BINOCULAR helps the restorer to examine the painting more closely. It allows him to see a three-dimensional image of the surface of the painting – he can see each brushstroke very clearly.

RELINING A PAINTING

Sometimes even the back of a painting needs restoring – when the canvas has weakened and is no longer able to support the paint. The HOT TABLE is then used to join the old painting to a new canvas lining with wax, using heat and pressure.

19

What is Tempera Paint?

Until the fifteenth century, when oil painting methods improved, most pictures were painted in tempera paint. There were many different ways of making it. One way was to mix the powdered pigments (made from coloured earth and minerals) with the yolk of an egg. This sticky paint mixture was then painted on to a wooden panel which had a specially prepared absorbent surface. (See pages 16–17.)

DO-IT-YOURSELF TEMPERA PAINT

What you will need:
1. a flat piece of wood or hardboard the size you want your picture to be
2. wood primer or undercoat
3. powder paints
4. an egg
5. vinegar
6. paint brushes, water

(Because tempera paint cracks easily, you will have to paint it on to a hard surface.)

1. Prepare the wood or hardboard. Make sure the surface is smooth and paint it with primer or undercoat. Leave until dry.
2. Break the egg into a bowl and add a tablespoonful of water and a drop of vinegar. Mix well.
3. Mix your powder colours using the egg mixture instead of water.

POINTS TO NOTICE
Although people used to use just the yolk of egg, you will get similar results using the whole egg and you will find it is less sticky to apply. Powder paint is made to be slightly sticky and most of the colours are made by chemical methods, but even so you will get some idea from this about old tempera painting methods.

(DON'T FORGET TO ASK BEFORE YOU TAKE ANYTHING FROM THE KITCHEN!)

What is Oil Paint?

Oil paint is made by mixing the same powdered pigments used in tempera paint with linseed oil and turpentine instead of egg and water.

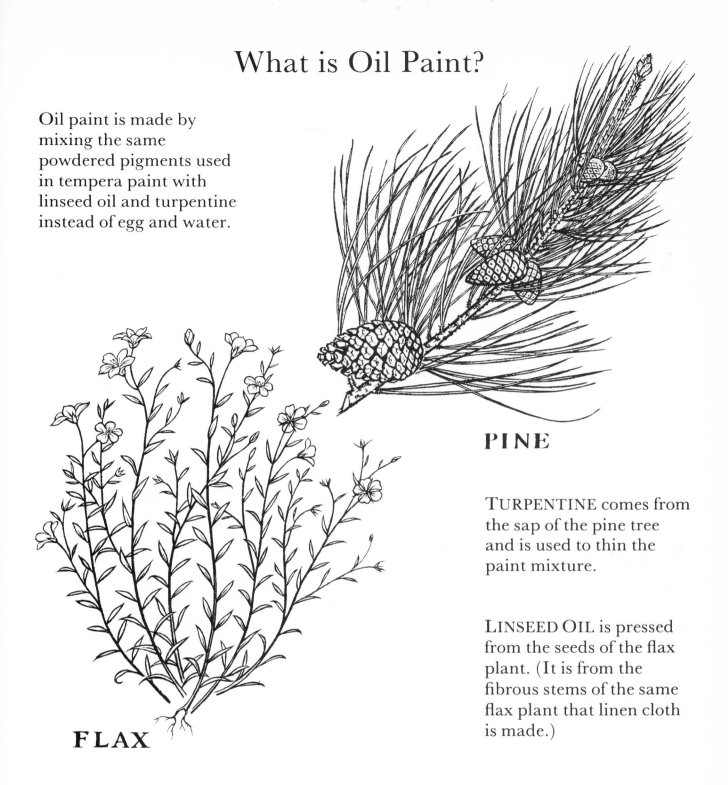

PINE

FLAX

TURPENTINE comes from the sap of the pine tree and is used to thin the paint mixture.

LINSEED OIL is pressed from the seeds of the flax plant. (It is from the fibrous stems of the same flax plant that linen cloth is made.)

Because it did not crack and flake off as easily as tempera paint, oil paint no longer had to be put on a stiff wooden panel but could be put on canvas.

Canvas paintings could then be as large as the piece of cloth coming from the weaver's loom – or even larger, if two pieces of cloth were sewn together.

Usually it was linen cloth (made from flax) that was stretched across the wooden frames to make the canvases on which the artist painted.

LEONARDO DA VINCI

The Virgin and Child with St. Anne and St. John the Baptist

You are looking at a piece of paper that is nearly 500 years old. Actually it's not one piece of paper but several pieces glued together. Look carefully – you can see the joins.

Show on the rectangle below where the joins in the paper appear.

The Virgin Mary

_____

Jesus

_____

Finish labelling the figures.

Who or what is the Virgin sitting on? _____

Which parts of the cartoon are unfinished? __
_____

This picture is really a kind of paper pattern called a CARTOON. (The word comes from the Italian *cartone* [say kar-tone-ay] meaning thick paper.) It is a design for a picture which Leonardo never painted – in fact he never even finished the cartoon.

Do you think the group is meant to be indoors or out of doors? _____
Say why. _____

How would you describe their clothes?
    close fitting? _____
    loose drapery? _____
    casual? _____
    smart? _____
    or what? _____

Which coloured chalks has the artist used? (Tick one or more.)
    green? _____
    blue? _____
    pale pink? _____
    brown? _____
    grey? _____
    white? _____
    black? _____
    yellow? _____
    purple? _____
    orange? _____

A drawing as large as this one is very rare – people usually threw them away when they had been used. But Leonardo was so famous and so much admired in his lifetime (1452–1519) that people treasured even quick sketches done by him – and lots of these have been saved.

Notice the way Leonardo has smudged the white chalk to make the light parts of the painting look soft.
Has he done this with the shadows as well? _____

Why do you think the picture is kept in a darkened room?

_____

How a Cartoon was Used

Find these two tiny works by the Italian painter Raphael (1483–1520). One is a cartoon, the other is a painting done from that cartoon. Look at the cartoon closely and you will see black pin pricks around the main figures.

1. The artist pricked holes around his design.
2. He put the cartoon over the canvas or wood he was going to paint on.
3. He dabbed black chalk through the holes so that the outlines on the cartoon appeared on the surface below.

ALLEGORY

This picture is called *An Allegory* (for an explanation of this word, see page 38).

But it has a second, more popular title: *Vision of a Knight*.

While the knight is asleep he has a dream or vision of the two ladies who are standing on either side of him. One holds a book and a sword – she stands in front of a hilly landscape. The other holds flowers and stands in front of a rich valley.

No one is sure who these people are meant to be or what the story is.

Can you make up one?

Who are the ladies? _____
_____

What objects are they holding and why? _____
_____

Will they still be there when the knight wakes?
_____

CARTOON

PAINTING

Make Your own Cartoon

What you will need:
1. a pin
2. tracing paper
   (greaseproof paper will
   do)
3. a sheet of white paper
4. black powder
   (try charcoal, soot or
   powder paint)
5. a paint brush or cotton
   wool

1. Trace this knight and
   his horse as carefully as
   you can.
2. Prick holes around
   your tracing of the
   knight, his horse and
   some details of the
   harness and armour.
   (Make sure you rest it
   on a suitable surface.)
3. Put your sheet of white
   paper under your sheet
   of tracing paper (the
   cartoon).
4. Dab the powdered
   charcoal through the
   holes. Use a brush or
   cotton wool. Be careful
   not to move the papers
   while you do it.
5. Remove the cartoon.
   Use a pencil to join up
   the dots.
6. Now you are ready to
   paint your picture.

The Modern Cartoon

SUBSTANCE AND SHADOW.

About 150 years ago the meaning of the word 'cartoon' changed. Designs submitted in a competition for wall paintings for the Houses of Parliament were mocked in the humorous magazine *Punch*. From this the word 'cartoon' got its new meaning of a humorous drawing.

Here is the first cartoon with the new meaning. It draws attention to the contrast between paintings of fat rich people and their pets and the thin poor people looking at them – not at all a funny subject to us nowadays.

26

MICHELANGELO *Entombment*

In 1506 this famous antique marble statue (below) was discovered in Rome. It is probably Greek and was made before Christ was born. People knew from ancient descriptions that it had once existed, so its discovery caused great excitement.

It shows a Trojan priest, Laocoön (say Lay-ok-ko-on), and his two sons being attacked by snakes.

Now look at the photograph of the statue and at Michelangelo's *Entombment*.

This picture by Michelangelo (1475–1564) is unfinished. Which parts are completed, which unfinished and which hardly started at all? _____

_____

The dead Jesus is being taken to His tomb. How do you know He is dead? _____

_____

What do you think Michelangelo was going to put in the bottom right-hand corner? _____

Is the tomb in:
   a hole in the ground? _____

   a church or chapel? _____
   a cave? _____
   or what? _____

Which of these statements do you think fits this picture?
1. The artist's style is rather sketchy. _____
2. The people in the picture look hard and shiny. _____
3. Michelangelo has used bright eye-catching colours. _____

Do you think Michelangelo had seen the Laocoön before he painted the picture in 1506? _____

Introducing the Four Evangelists

The life of Jesus Christ is recorded in four books of the New Testament known as the Gospels. The writers of the Gospels were called the four Evangelists (which is Greek for bringers of good news). They are usually shown with (or as) winged creatures. This idea comes from a vision seen by the Prophet Ezekiel described in the Old Testament (Book of Ezekiel, chapter 1, verses 5–14).

ST. MATTHEW is often shown with a little man with wings because he wrote about Christ as a man. He is often shown with his book and sometimes with money, as he was a tax collector earlier in his life.

(Label the figures.)

ST. MARK is often shown with a winged lion. He may have a pen and a book too.

ST. LUKE is usually shown with a winged ox, the symbol of sacrifice. He may hold a book or be shown painting the Virgin Mary. He is the patron saint of painters.

ST. JOHN THE EVANGELIST is usually shown with an eagle (symbol of high inspiration) and a book. He may also have a goblet with a snake in it, which refers to an attempt made to poison him.

(Look for the Evangelists in paintings in the Gallery. If you have any difficulty, see page 62.)

Decorating the Vatican

Pope Julius II was Pope from 1503 to 1513. He loved paintings and commissioned many famous artists to produce works for him in Rome. It was for him that Michelangelo painted the ceiling of the Sistine Chapel and Raphael painted the rooms in the Vatican known as the Stanze.

RAPHAEL

Portrait of Pope Julius II

HOW THE NATIONAL GALLERY DISCOVERED A PAINTING BY RAPHAEL

In 1824 the English government bought thirty-eight paintings from the collection of John Julius Angerstein, a banker who had died the year before.

The works were shown in Angerstein's former town house (100 Pall Mall), and this was the beginning of the National Gallery collection.

100 Pall Mall, the original National Gallery

Among those thirty-eight pictures was one of Pope Julius II. When it was bought it looked very dark and dingy. After several hundred years pictures become covered with dirt.

Just think of the soot that candles and oil lamps must have given off before the discovery of electricity.

Other versions of the picture looked almost exactly the same, and experts thought that the one in the National Gallery was just another copy of the lost original. The picture was on view in the lower floor galleries, where the less important paintings are hung.

Then in 1970 it was decided that the picture should be
1. cleaned and
2. X-rayed

Did the X-ray show A or B? _____

When experts X-ray a picture they can see where the artist made alterations. They can see what his original intentions were and how he changed his mind.

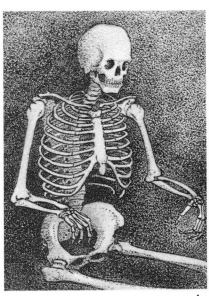

A

B

If you are copying someone else's picture you do it exactly – you don't need to make changes. So changes and alterations which are revealed by an X-ray may tell us that a picture is an original.

HOLBEIN
The Ambassadors

These two French men visited London in the year 1533. The one on the left was an official visitor to the court of Henry VIII. While he was in England he was joined by his friend. Hans Holbein (1497–1543), a German artist working in England, painted this portrait of them.

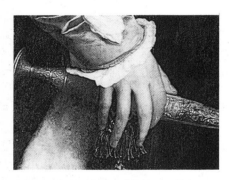

The picture is full of hidden references – for example, the artist has hidden the ages of the two men in the picture.

Can you find their ages?

Look carefully at the dagger case the man on the left is holding, and the book the other is leaning on. Holbein has written *aetatis suae* (Latin for 'his age') and then a number.

Write in their ages (if you can read them) here: _____ and _____
(The answer is on page 62 if you have difficulty.)

Also hidden in the picture is a Crucifix (the image of Christ on the Cross).

Where is it? _____

The man on the left was called Jean de Dinteville.

What is odd about his red shirt? _____
_____

What is the lining of his surcoat made of? _____

What is on the medal he is wearing round his neck?
_____

Why do you think Georges de Selve (on the right) is dressed so differently?
1. He was on his way to bed in his dressing gown? _____
2. He was in mourning for a dead friend or relation? _____
3. He was a bishop or priest? _____

WHAT IS THE MYSTERIOUS OBJECT ON THE FLOOR?

If you are in the Gallery, look at the picture from the right-hand side.

Or, hold this book upright and look at the picture sideways from the place marked at the edge of page 33.

Can you see now that it looks like this → and is actually a picture of a _____ ?

32

Look from here

Would you say that this
painting shows the men:
    larger than life? _____
    smaller than life? _____
    or about life size? _____

Are they looking at you?

WHAT TIME IS IT?

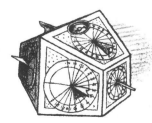 

Amongst the objects on
the shelves are
instruments for measuring
dates and times. They
show 11 April, 10.30 a.m.
– but you have to be an
expert to read them.

33

The Ambassadors' Objects

The objects on the shelves show the interests of the men.
Tick which of these you can see:

lute

tape measure

celestial globe

violin

terrestrial globe

candlestick

clock

shell

pair of scissors

cylindrical sundial

flutes in a case

torquetum
(for working out the
position of stars and
planets)

mathematics book

bowl of fruit

music book

polyhedral sundial

Do you know what these
words mean?
CYLINDRICAL = in the
shape of a cylinder
POLYHEDRAL = with
many sides
TERRESTRIAL = of the
Earth
CELESTIAL = of the
heavens

Perspective Pictures

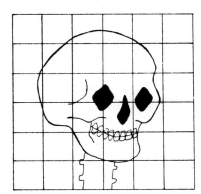

Make your own perspective picture like the skull in Holbein's *Ambassadors*. Here's how it's done

Here is a skull drawn on a grid.

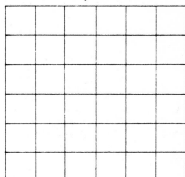

Draw your own face on the blank grid.

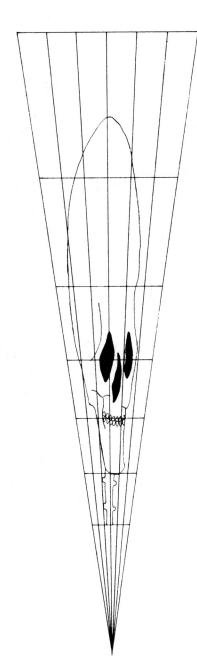

Here the shape of the grid has changed, and the skull has been changed with it.

Re-draw your face in this distorted grid. Make sure you elongate your picture to fit the new shapes.

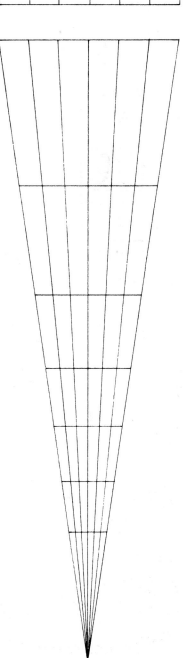

Hold the book flat and look along the page here.

35

BRONZINO

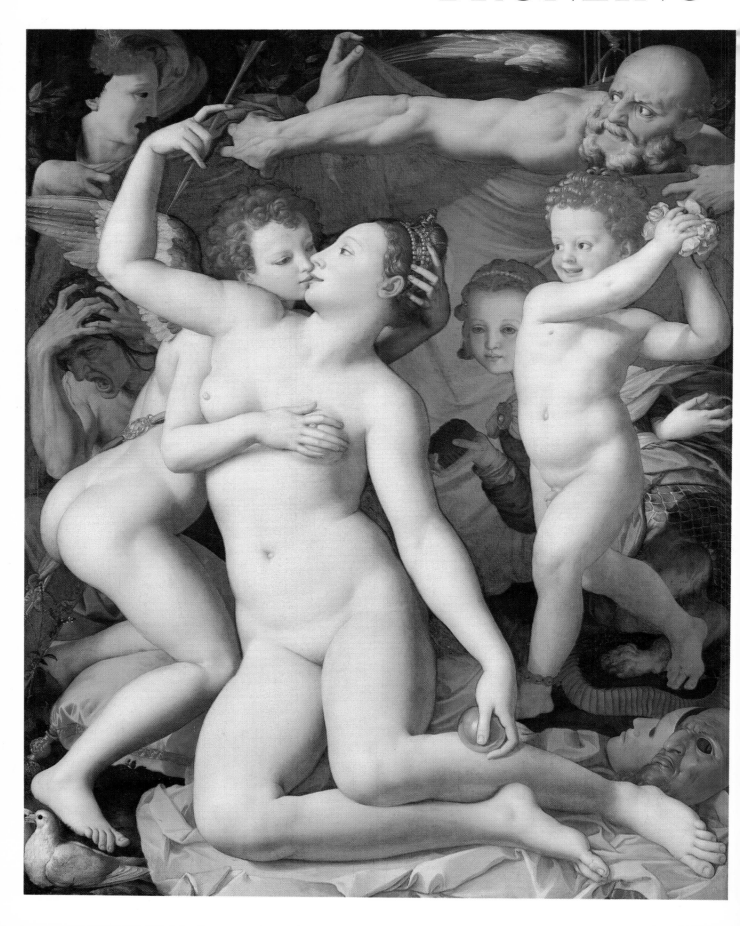

Allegory with Venus and Cupid

DO YOU THINK THIS PICTURE IS RUDE?

At different times in the past people have been offended by pictures of naked figures.

When Bronzino (1503–72) painted this picture in about 1545 it probably would not have been thought offensive.

However, between the time it was painted and 1860, when it was bought by the National Gallery, someone clearly thought it was. So three alterations were made.

Compare this photograph with the one on the facing page – or better still with the original painting.

Can you spot the three changes?

_____
_____
_____

The painting was cleaned in 1958 and the additions were removed.

Most of these objects are in the painting. Tick them off when you have seen them. Underline any you *cannot* see.

scythe _____
cushion _____
bells _____
watering can _____
thorns _____

pearls _____
roses _____
golden ball _____
doves _____
jewels _____
masks _____
honeycomb _____
arrow _____
hourglass _____
cheesegrater _____

Who's Who

A picture (or piece of writing) which is full of hidden meaning, like Bronzino's painting, is called an ALLEGORY. No one is really sure of the exact meaning of this Allegory by Bronzino. However, we think we know who the main characters are. Can you identify them all? Sketch them in the boxes provided.

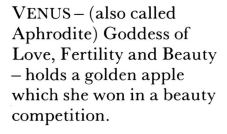

VENUS – (also called Aphrodite) Goddess of Love, Fertility and Beauty – holds a golden apple which she won in a beauty competition.

TIME – (also called Cronus or Saturn) – is usually shown as a winged man carrying an hourglass and sometimes a scythe.

JEALOUSY – tears her hair.

CUPID – (also called Amor and Eros) son of Venus – is usually shown as a winged boy carrying a bow and arrows. The touch of one of his arrows would cause his victim to fall in love – and he used to shoot his arrows carelessly at gods and humans alike. He never grew up.

FOLLY – here throws rose petals. He has bells round one ankle and seems unaware of the thorns which pierce his foot.

PLEASURE (or is she FRAUD?) – holds a honeycomb in one hand and the sting from her tail in the other.

OBLIVION – helps Time to pull the blue cloth over the kissing couple.

Vices in Modern Dress

Here are some vices:
Pride
Greed

Anger
Laziness

Draw or paint what you
think they would look like
as people today.

Can you put them all in
one picture?

REMBRANDT

There once was a wicked King of Babylon called Belshazzar. One night, when he was feasting with his friends (using gold and silver cups stolen from the Temple of Solomon) a mysterious hand suddenly appeared & wrote a message on the wall. The king was mystified and very frightened. He sent for Daniel, a Jewish exile at the Babylonian court, who told him that the writing said that Belshazzar had been 'weighed in the balances and found wanting' (in other words he was not good enough) & that the Kingdom of Babylon would fall & that Belshazzar would die. That night the king was killed and Darius the Persian took the kingdom.

Belshazzar's Feast

During the 1630s (when this picture was painted) Rembrandt's career was going well – he earned a lot of money and began to enjoy living expensively. He used to buy exotic objects from junk shops and markets and he sometimes included these in his paintings. Perhaps he owned some of the clothes and jewels in *Belshazzar's Feast*.

The National Gallery has about twenty works by Rembrandt. Look at a few others.

Can you say which colours Rembrandt used most?

_____
_____
_____
_____

Can you find any picture by him with much blue or green in it? _____
_____

The writing in *Belshazzar's Feast* is in Hebrew. The original story comes from the Bible – Book of Daniel, chapter 5.

What time of day do you think it is? _____
Why? _____
_____

Where is most of the light coming from?
    a candle? _____
    a window? _____
    flaming torches? _____
    the mysterious writing?
    _____

or where? _____

List the things you can see that are made of gold or silver:

_____
_____
_____
_____
_____
_____

Are the people you can see at Belshazzar's table mostly men or mostly women? _____

Do you think this is the beginning or the end of the meal? _____
Why? _____
_____

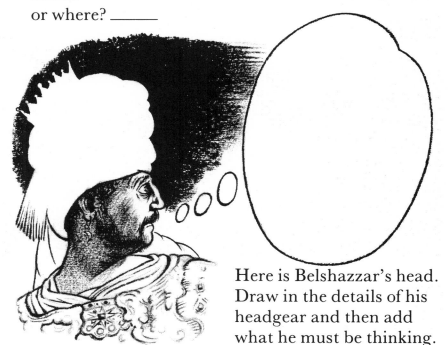

Here is Belshazzar's head. Draw in the details of his headgear and then add what he must be thinking.

Does he seem:
    excited? _____
    sleepy? _____
    bored? _____
    hungry? _____
    surprised? _____
    happy? _____
    frightened? _____
    full? _____
    or what? _____

Self-Portraits

When a person paints a picture of himself (or herself) it is called a SELF-PORTRAIT. At the bottom of this page are three self-portraits to be seen in the National Gallery. Look at them. What different methods have the artists used to tell you about themselves?

At home, look in a mirror. How are you feeling today?

cheerful? _____
angry? _____
sad? _____
giggly? _____
or what? _____

Make a face that shows how you feel and draw your self-portrait in this empty frame. Then add one or two objects that will tell people in 300 years' time a bit more about yourself.

Salvator Rosa

Elisabeth Vigée-LeBrun

Bartolomé Murillo

42

Portraits of Rembrandt

1640

1669

Rembrandt van Rijn (1606–69) was the greatest Dutch painter of the seventeenth century. He spent much of his working life in Amsterdam and died there at the age of 63. Amongst other things, he painted over sixty self-portraits – the National Gallery has two.
Can you find them?

This one was painted in the year 1640.
How old was he in that year? _____

This one was painted in the year he died. At this time he was poor and lonely (most of his close family and friends had already died).

How has he shown this in the painting? _____
_____

How many years passed between the painting of these two portraits? _____

In which of the two does he look happier and more prosperous? _____

Find Rembrandt's signature inside the cover.

43

Flowers in a Terracotta Vase

Jan Van Huysum (1682–1749) was a Dutch flower painter. Many artists of the period, including his own father, painted pictures of flowers. This type of picture is called a STILL LIFE.

A still life usually shows an arrangement of inanimate objects – objects which cannot move. But very often the artist surprises us by hiding little living creatures among the plants and flowers.

Not all the flowers in the vase were in season when the artist began painting, probably during the summer, so he had to wait until the following spring to finish the painting.

He then put both dates on the picture.

Can you find them?

_____

and_____

List the objects in this picture which in reality _can_ move:

_____
_____
_____
_____
_____
_____

Is the flower vase seen from:
   above? _____
   below? _____
   or straight on? _____

Write down the colours of the striped tulips.

_____

and _____

How many striped tulips can you see here? _____

Which fruit do you think looks most appetising?

_____

Which six of the following are _not_ included?
   caterpillar? _____
   walnut? _____
   daffodil? _____
   spider? _____
   waterdrop? _____
   lizard? _____
   ladybird? _____
   snail? _____

Tulipomania

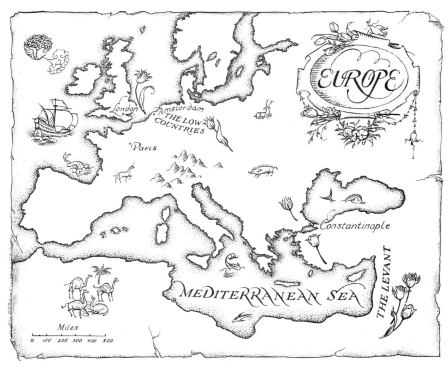

The Strange Story of Striped Tulips

The tulip is not a native plant of Northern Europe – it was first brought to the Low Countries (the Netherlands, Belgium and Luxembourg) in the sixteenth century from Constantinople and the Levant (those countries bordering on the Eastern Mediterranean). Its early flowering and rich and splendid colours soon made it the most fashionable flower of the time.

Tulip bulbs varied in price according to the colour and type of flower. Single colours were quite cheap – but striped tulips were in great demand and became very expensive. Prices reached fantastic levels, and there are stories of farmers exchanging a whole farm for a single bulb.

Exotic sea shells were also highly prized. They were brought from the East Indies where the Dutch had colonies. Look out for them in Dutch paintings of the seventeenth century.

Tulip Vase. Hampton Court

Look out for Tulip Vases

In the seventeenth century people began to make special vases to display their precious tulips. You can sometimes see these in museums or grand country houses. They look like the one illustrated here, and were usually of blue and white china, patterned to make them look Chinese. Curiously enough, no one is sure whether they were for cut tulips or whether tulip bulbs were grown in them!

46

A Page of Flowers

Flowers, trees and other plants are often found in paintings because they have special meanings. Here are a few of these meanings. Look out for these plants in National Gallery paintings and make a note of where you find them. Keep a look out for them in other art galleries too.

The LILY is a symbol of purity. It is often found in pictures of the Virgin Mary. Various saints who led very pure lives are shown with lilies too – for example, St. Dominic.
I found a lily in a painting called _____
by _____

The IRIS is often found in pictures of the Virgin Mary instead of, or with, the lily. This may be because the Germans call it a 'sword lily'.
I found an iris in a painting called _____
by _____

The name COLUMBINE comes from the Latin word *columba*, meaning dove, because when seen from certain angles it looks like a dove in flight. The dove is a symbol of the Holy Spirit, so this flower has the same meaning.
I found a columbine in a painting called _____
by _____

The DAISY is a symbol of innocence and is often used in pictures of the baby Jesus.
I found a daisy in a painting called _____
by _____

Daisy

Columbine

Lily

Iris

(If you have difficulty in finding these, see page 62 for a list of a few paintings in which they appear.)

An Allegory with Venus and Time

This painting was once part of the decoration of a ceiling. It was painted by the Venetian artist Tiepolo (1696–1770), and it used to be in a palace owned by the Contarini family – one of the oldest and richest in Venice.

Where is this scene taking place?
in a forest? _____
on top of a mountain? _____
up in the sky? _____
or where? _____

Look carefully at the baby which is being presented to the Goddess of Love, Venus, by Time.

What is odd about the baby's right arm? _____
_____

Do you think it is a good-looking child? _____

Or is it rather ugly? _____

Is Time young or old? _____

Tick which of the following Time has with him:

hourglass _____

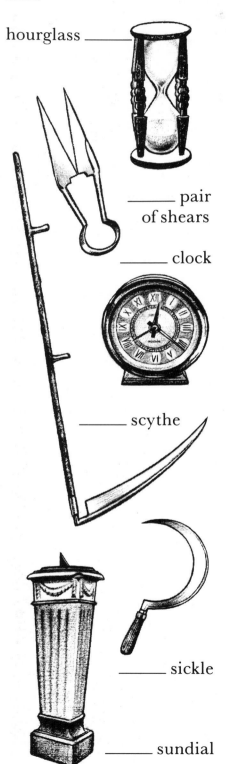

_____ pair of shears

_____ clock

_____ scythe

_____ sickle

_____ sundial

Venus's son Cupid is usually shown with wings and a bow and arrow.

Which does he have here?
_____

Tick which parts of his body you can see:
navel? _____
nose? _____
left hand? _____
right hand? _____
bottom? _____
mouth? _____
soles of feet? _____
eyes? _____

What are the girls about to throw at Venus? _____

Are the doves
fighting? _____
kissing? _____
or what? _____

Experts do not agree about the true meaning of this painting or about who the baby is.

Can *you* guess who it is?

Decorating a Ceiling

Have a look at the ceilings in your home.

Are there any paintings on them? _____

If not, why not design one?

1. Choose which room you feel needs a painted ceiling most.
2. Choose a subject that you think would suit that room – for example, sky and clouds might look nice in a bathroom or a navy blue ceiling with moon and stars in a bedroom.
3. Draw or paint your idea on a small scale *on a piece of paper*.
4. Be as imaginative as you can and remember that everything you show should be *seen from below*.
5. Don't be surprised if the grown-ups in the house are not very keen on you painting the actual ceiling. You may have to wait until you are grown up and own a room of your own before you can put your ideas into practice!

A Page of Odd Saints

ST. LUCY (who was a Christian) had beautiful eyes. One young man was so obsessed by them that he could get no rest. So Lucy tore them out of her head and sent them to him. Amazed by her courage and full of remorse, he too became a Christian.

ST. ANTHONY ABBOT became a hermit for twenty years, denying himself all worldly goods. He lived to be 105 years old and is often shown with a crutch. He carries a bell to exorcise demons, and a pig accompanies him to represent the sensuality and gluttony he overcame.

(Label the figures.)

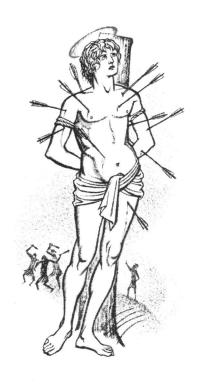

ST. AGATHA was a beautiful Christian woman whose breasts were cut off and who was thrown into a fire by an enraged suitor to whom she refused to give herself. When a volcano threatened to erupt, her veil was used to stop it.

ST. SEBASTIAN was a Roman guardsman and a secret Christian. When this was discovered he was bound to a stake, shot with arrows and left for dead. A lady tended his wounds and he recovered, but the Emperor was furious and had him clubbed to death.

(Look for these Odd Saints in paintings in the Gallery. If you have difficulty, see page 62.)

CONSTABLE

Today John Constable (1776–1836) is one of the most popular of all English painters. He specialised in natural looking landscapes, and he paid great attention to light effects and to the sky and clouds. This is probably his best-known and best-loved painting.

But in 1821 when it was finished Constable was not popular and he had difficulty in finding anyone to buy it. It was sold three years later, in 1824, for £400. Today it is priceless.

The title *The Hay Wain* is really a nickname. Constable called his picture one of the following. Can you tell which? (Answer on page 62.)

Landscape: Early Morning _____

Landscape: Noon _____
Landscape: Evening _____
Landscape: Night _____
The Chariot Race _____

The Hay Wain

Above is a modern photograph of the same view painted by Constable.

Compare the photograph with Constable's view.

In what ways is it different?

_____

Do you think Constable altered what he saw in order to make his picture look better? _____

If so, what do you think he altered? _____
_____
_____

What do you think this view will look like in another 150 years?

List a few things which might then be found in the scene – for example, a motorway, a tower block, an aeroplane etc.

_____
_____
_____

Pentimenti

ANSWER THESE QUESTIONS IN FRONT OF CONSTABLE'S HAY WAIN

The hay wain is the hay cart in the stream.

Why do you think it is there?
1. The horses are having a drink and cooling their legs? _____
2. The driver is drunk? _____
3. They are crossing the stream? _____
4. They are lost? _____
5. Or why? _____

How many people are near the stream? _____

What are they doing?
_____
_____

What are the men in the background doing?
    playing cricket? _____
    playing football? _____
    hay-making? _____
    nothing – they are asleep? _____

FIND THE GHOST

Just in front of the dog's nose there is the ghostly shape of a boy and a barrel. Constable put them in at first – but then changed his mind and painted them out.

Oil paint slowly becomes more and more transparent with age. So Constable's boy and barrel are gradually becoming visible again.

Art historians have a special word for alterations like these: PENTIMENTI.

Did you notice the *pentimenti* in *The Arnolfini Marriage* (page 10)? (Look at the man's feet.)

Constable changed his mind more than once. Here is a detail of a full-size sketch he made for *The Hay Wain*. It is different from both the finished picture and the 'ghost'.

What does it show? _____
_____
_____
_____

Detail of oil sketch for *The Hay Wain*.
Victoria and Albert Museum

An Odd Page of Saints

ST. JOHN THE BAPTIST is often shown dressed in a kind of tunic made from camel's hair. He foretold the coming of Christ and is usually shown carrying a lamb, which is a symbol of Christ – 'The Lamb of God'. Can you find him in two of the paintings in this book? (Answer on page 62.)

ST. MARY MAGDALENE was a sinner who repented. She can be recognised by the jar of ointment with which she anointed Christ's feet.

(Label the figures.)

ST. FRANCIS OF ASSISI founded the Franciscan Order of Friars, whose rules include humility and absolute poverty. He is usually shown in the brown habit of this Order and may have wounds on his hands and feet, in sympathy with the wounds of Christ.

ST. GEORGE is the patron saint of England. The story of how he killed a dragon and saved a princess is well known. Many artists painted it – see how many pictures of the subject you can find in the National Gallery.

(Look for these Saints in the Gallery. If you have difficulty in finding them, see page 62.)

Cloud Studies

Here are two studies Constable made of clouds. He painted them very quickly out of doors and then noted the date, time and wind direction on the back.

Try drawing clouds – it's not as easy as you might think!

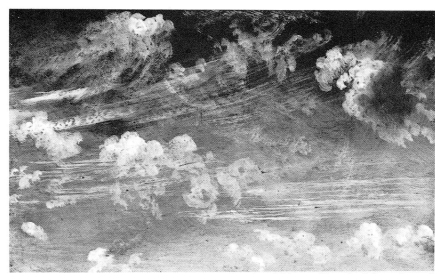

Study of Cirrus Clouds. Victoria and Albert Museum

Sept 5. 1822. Looking S.E. noon. Wind very brisk, & effect bright & fresh. Clouds — moving very fast — with occasional very bright openings to the blue.

Study of Clouds and inscription from back. Victoria and Albert Museum

A Page of Plants

The ROSE has many meanings: victory, pride and love being three. It is the flower of Venus, Goddess of Love. In Christian pictures the red rose is a symbol of a martyr and the white rose is a symbol of purity.
I found a rose in a painting called _____ by _____

The PALM frond was a symbol of victory in Roman times. But in paintings it usually means that the person holding one is a martyr (one who died for his or her beliefs) and so won victory over death.
I found a palm in a painting called _____ by _____

The DANDELION is a bitter herb. It is used as a symbol of grief.
I found a dandelion in a painting called _____ by_____

The ORANGE tree is a symbol of purity, chastity and generosity. That is why orange blossom is worn by brides.
I found an orange in a painting called _____ by_____

(*If you have difficulty in finding these, see page 62 for a list of a few paintings in which they appear.*)

Creepy Crawlies

If you look carefully at paintings you will often find that the artist has put in tiny details that you did not notice at first glance. Sometimes these are there to add extra meaning to the picture – for example, the creepy crawlies on this page have special symbolic meanings. When you are at the National Gallery, look for these in the paintings.

The BEE is a symbol of hard work and good order and, because it produces honey, of sweetness as well.

The SPIDER sucks the blood from the insects it catches in its web. It is the symbol of a miser who will become rich at the expense of others. It may also symbolise the Devil, who also traps his victims. The cobweb stands for human frailty and weakness.

This type of scallop or COCKLE SHELL is the symbol of a pilgrim. Pilgrims used to carry scallops to use as water scoops. St. James the Great, the pilgrim saint, is often shown with one.

The life-cycle of the BUTTERFLY goes from egg to caterpillar to chrysalis to adult. At the chrysalis stage it appears to be dead, until the adult insect emerges. Therefore the butterfly has become a symbol of life after death and of the Resurrection.

FLIES carry dirt and disease. They may be used to symbolise Sin. A fly may be shown settled on a portrait – it may be there to tell us that the person portrayed was dead, or just to make him (or her) look more real.

The SCORPION'S sting is at the end of its tail, and can cause great agony often followed by death. The scorpion is a symbol of evil – and in particular of traitors, such as Judas. It is sometimes found on the flags and shields of the soldiers who arrested Christ.

People used to think that SNAILS were born in mud and would then feed upon it. They therefore are symbols of laziness in particular (also perhaps because they are so slow) and of sin in general.

ROUSSEAU
Tropical Storm with a Tiger

Henri Rousseau (1844–1910) was nicknamed *le Douanier*, which is French for 'the customs officer' – he worked in a toll station for many years. He used to paint pictures like this one in his spare time. He claimed he had been in Mexico with the French army in the 1860s, and it was there that he had seen tropical forests and exotic animals. This story may not be true – he could have worked from photographs and made visits to the zoo.

Rousseau called this picture *Surprised!*
Do you think this is a better title than the one it now has? _____
Think of another title for it and write it below.

_____

Tiger Cut-out

TIGER INSTRUCTIONS

1.

2.

3.

KEY

━━━ cut

──── fold down

- - - - fold up

CUB

Trace the mother tiger and her cub (or put carbon paper and your work paper underneath and go over the outlines).

Then cut out the animals to the instructions above. You can make twin cubs by tracing the cub pattern twice.

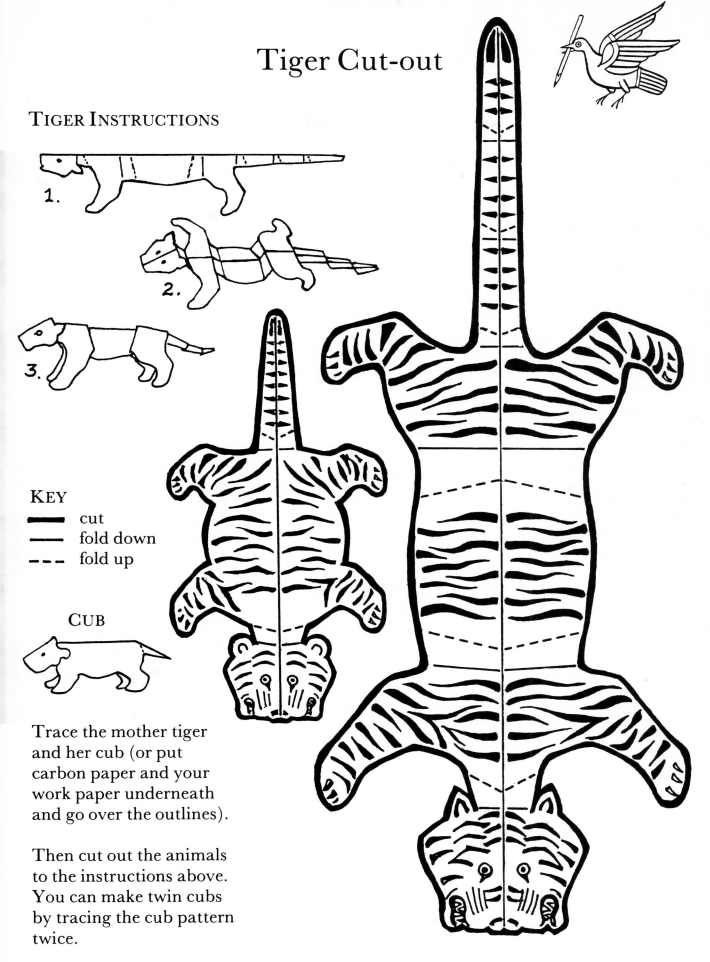

Answers

page 6
Richard II was 10 years old when he became King.
page 7
The baby's halo is decorated with prickly thorns (the Crown of
    Thorns).
page 11
If you look carefully, you can see 4 people reflected in the
    mirror.
The one candle (which is alight) represents divine light because
    the ceremony is a holy one, or it may be a clock – no one is
    absolutely certain.
page 23
The Virgin is sitting on the lap of her mother, St. Anne.
The feet and hands of the two women are unfinished.
Leonardo has also smudged the dark chalk in the shadows.
    This technique has a name – SFUMATO (say sphoo-ma-toe).
The cartoon is kept in a darkened room because it is so delicate
    that strong light could damage it.
page 32
The ages of the two men are 29 and 25.
The crucifix is in the upper left-hand corner, at the edge of the
    curtain.
Jean de Dinteville wears a medal showing the Archangel
    Michael slaying a dragon.
Georges de Selve is dressed so differently because he was a
    bishop or a priest.
page 33
The men are shown about life-size.
They are looking straight at you – wherever you stand!
page 41
Rembrandt used a lot of gold and red and yellow and brown.
He rarely used blue or green.
page 43
Rembrandt was 34 when the top self-portrait was painted.
In the bottom portrait he no longer wears the fancy costume of
    a rich man but a simple coat and work hat.
Between the painting of the two self-portraits 29 years had
    passed.
page 45
Jan Van Huysum painted the still life in 1736 and 1737.
page 49
The scene is taking place in the sky – but, of course; it is a
    ceiling decoration.
The baby's right arm is smaller than the left.
We hope the doves are kissing.
page 52
Constable called the painting *Landscape: Noon*.
The hay wain may be crossing the stream or it may just be
    stopped there to give the horses a drink and cool their legs.
The men in the background are hay-making.

If you have any difficulty in locating paintings that picture
various flowers, fruits, saints and creepy crawlies, the following
list will help you to find one of each. But there are are many
more in the Gallery – KEEP LOOKING.

page 14
CHERRY: *The Holy Family* by the Master of the Death of the
    Virgin
POMEGRANATE: *The Virgin and Child with a Pomegranate* by the
    studio of Botticelli
APPLE: *The Annunciation* by Carlo Crivelli
GRAPES: *The Supper at Emmaus* by Caravaggio
page 28
ST. MATTHEW: *St. Matthew, St. Catherine and St. John the
    Evangelist* by Stephan Lochner
ST. MARK: *The "Madonna of Humility"* by Lorenzo Veneziano
ST. LUKE: *St. Luke Painting the Virgin and Child* by a follower of
    Quentin Massys
ST. JOHN THE EVANGELIST: *St. John on the Island of Patmos* by
    Velázquez
page 47
LILY: *St. Dominic* by Giovanni Bellini
IRIS: *The Virgin and Child ("The Madonna with the Iris")* in the
    style of Albrecht Dürer
COLUMBINE: *The Virgin and Child with Saints and Donor* by David
DAISY: *Virgin and Child Enthroned* by Carlo Crivelli
page 51
ST. LUCY: *Holy Family with St. Lucy, another Female Saint and a
    Donor* by Cariani
ST. ANTHONY ABBOT: *The Virgin and Child with St. George and St.
    Anthony Abbot* by Pisanello
ST. AGATHA: *A Lady as St. Agatha* by Sebastiano del Piombo
ST. SEBASTIAN: *The Martyrdom of St. Sebastian* by Antonio and
    Piero del Pollaiuolo
page 55
ST. JOHN THE BAPTIST: *The Baptism of Christ* by Piero della
    Francesca. In this book, he is on page 6 and page 22.
ST. MARY MAGDALENE: *The Magdalen Reading* by Rogier van
    der Weyden
ST. FRANCIS OF ASSISI: *The Altarpiece of S. Francesco* by Sassetta
ST. GEORGE: *St. George and the Dragon* by Paolo Uccello
page 57
ROSE: *The Virgin and Child with Flowers* by Carlo Dolci
PALM: *Madonna and Child with St. Hippolytus and St. Catherine of
    Alexandria* by Moretto da Brescia
DANDELION: *St. Catherine of Alexandria* by Raphael
ORANGE: *The Holy Family with St. John* by Mantegna
pages 58–59
FLY: *St. Jerome in Penitence* by Sodoma
BEE: *Cupid Complaining to Venus* by Lucas Cranach
COCKLE SHELL: *The Walk to Emmaus* by Altobello Melone
BUTTERFLY: *Flowers in a Glass Vase* by Jacob van Walscappelle
SPIDER: We can't find one: can you?
SCORPION: *Scenes from the Life of St. John the Evangelist* by
    Giovanni del Ponte
SNAIL: *Virgin and Child Enthroned* by Carlo Crivelli

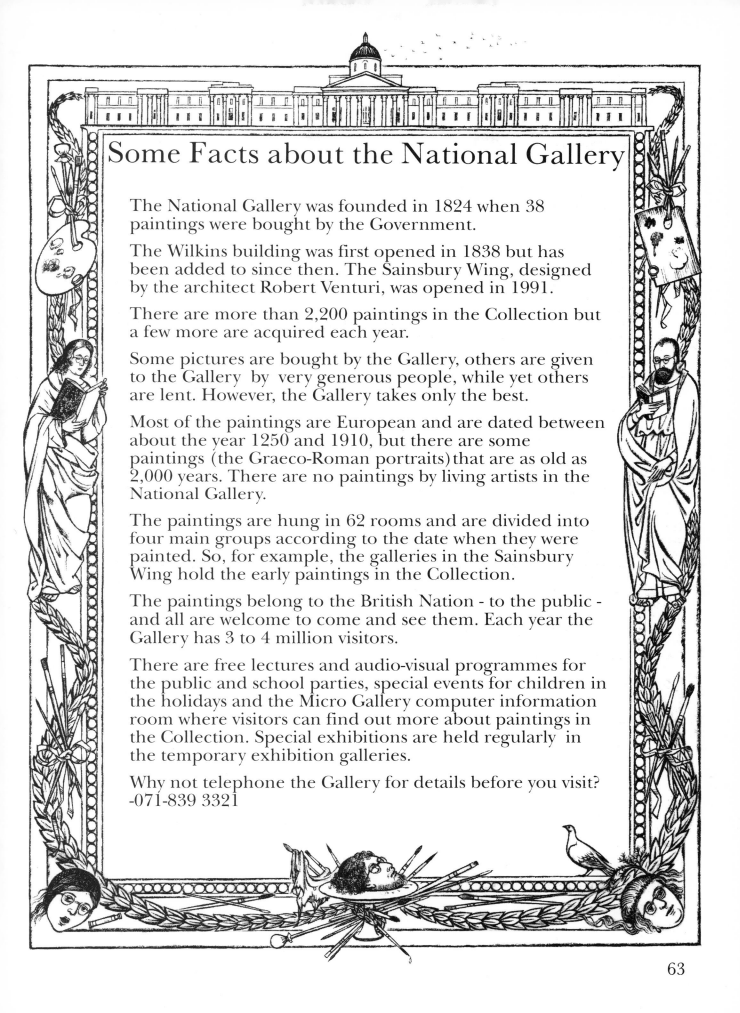

Some Facts about the National Gallery

The National Gallery was founded in 1824 when 38 paintings were bought by the Government.

The Wilkins building was first opened in 1838 but has been added to since then. The Sainsbury Wing, designed by the architect Robert Venturi, was opened in 1991.

There are more than 2,200 paintings in the Collection but a few more are acquired each year.

Some pictures are bought by the Gallery, others are given to the Gallery by very generous people, while yet others are lent. However, the Gallery takes only the best.

Most of the paintings are European and are dated between about the year 1250 and 1910, but there are some paintings (the Graeco-Roman portraits) that are as old as 2,000 years. There are no paintings by living artists in the National Gallery.

The paintings are hung in 62 rooms and are divided into four main groups according to the date when they were painted. So, for example, the galleries in the Sainsbury Wing hold the early paintings in the Collection.

The paintings belong to the British Nation - to the public - and all are welcome to come and see them. Each year the Gallery has 3 to 4 million visitors.

There are free lectures and audio-visual programmes for the public and school parties, special events for children in the holidays and the Micro Gallery computer information room where visitors can find out more about paintings in the Collection. Special exhibitions are held regularly in the temporary exhibition galleries.

Why not telephone the Gallery for details before you visit? -071-839 3321

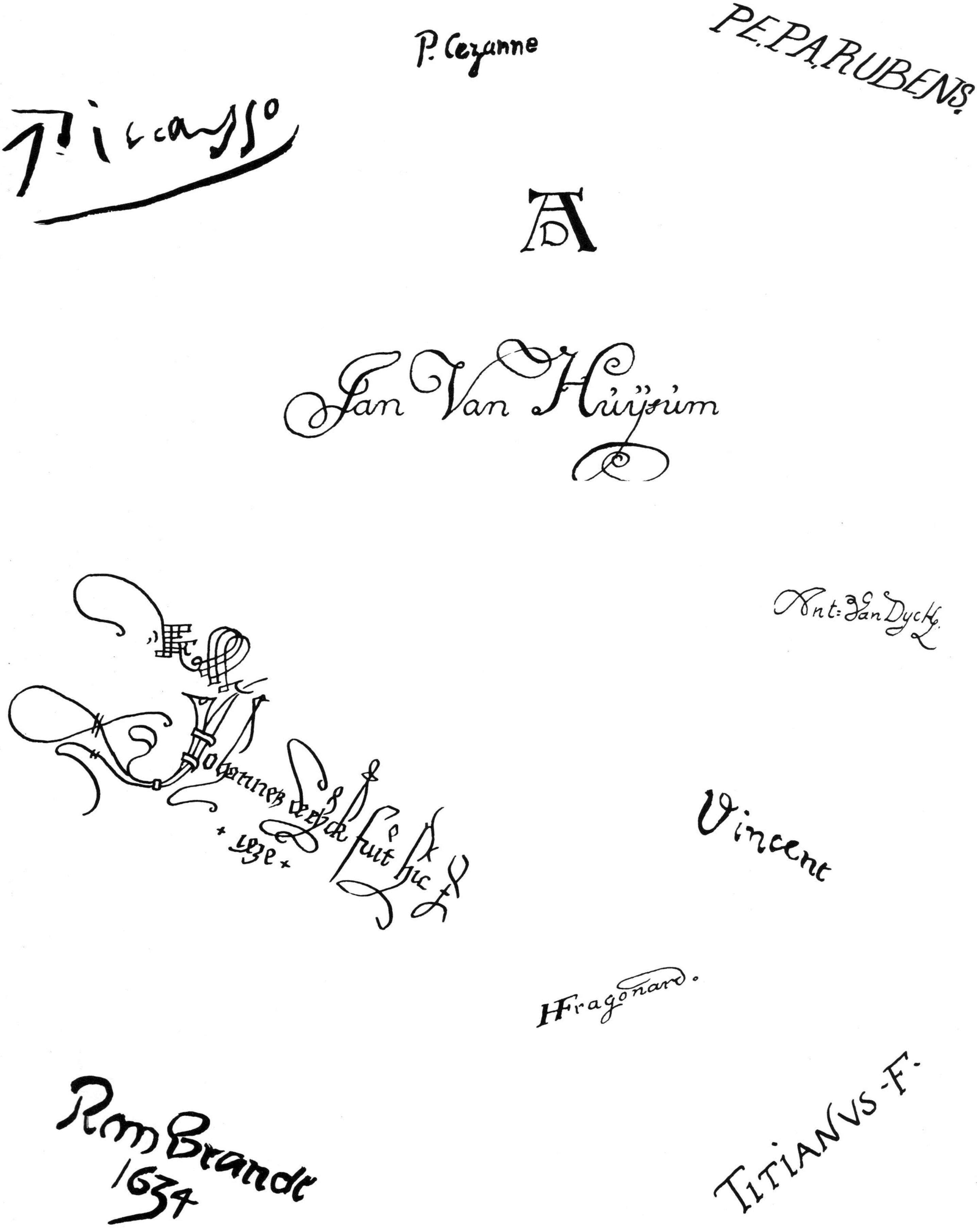

P. Cezanne

P.P.A.RUBENS.

Picasso

AD

Jan Van Huijsum

Ant: Van Dyck.

Johannes de Eyck fuit hic
1434

Vincent

H Fragonard.

Rembrandt
1634

TITIANVS·F·